What's cooking?

Crafty Cooking

BEGINNER'S BLUE BOOK

© Naumann & Göbel Verlagsgesellschaft mbH, a subsidiary of
VEMAG Verlags- und Medien Aktiengesellschaft, Cologne
www.apollo-intermedia.de

Complete production: Naumann & Göbel Verlagsgesellschaft mbH, Cologne
Printed in Germany

ISBN 3-625-10930-1

What's cooking?

Crafty Cooking
BEGINNER'S BLUE BOOK

NAUMANN & GÖBEL

Contents

Crafty Cooking

Let's get cooking, that is our motto! Do not let yourself be intimidated by pompousness, people talking shop and secretiveness. You see: it all happens in the kitchen and nobody is a lost case – honestly! You, too, can reap the glory normally reserved for the usual suspects – all you need are proper instructions to get cooking. We show you how to disentangle yourself from the kitchen chaos, get rid of those niggling doubts and create proper compositions. We will explain how to uncover a kitchen's secrets step by step.

Scared?

"I can't cook". The first step is always the hardest. This book will help you to get over this sentence – literally. Only very few people have either a genuine talent or have cooking in their genes. What you really need to cook properly are ideas, a touch of fantasy and sometimes patience. The rest is made up of experience and to a greater degree good tips and tricks and tried and tested recipes. Also, while curiosity might kill the cat, it is extremely useful in the kitchen.

While eating is really nothing more than ingesting food, all the things that go with it such as cooking, inviting and eating together etc. are social activities that can get as far as being a demanding hobby. To whichever degree you get involved, it should always be a creative challenge. So grab hold of the wooden spoon and get cooking! Because cooking is one thing and one thing only: fun! And the beauty is, it need neither be complicated nor costly. There are countless possibilities to still even the greatest hunger, the quick appetite or the need for something fancy – even if you do not have a lot to spare (time and money). And anything you make at home is more than just a trifle healthier than what is on offer in your local chippy or the fast food restaurant next door.

"But how can I possibly succeed?" Which pot, what utensils should you have, how do you prepare your kitchen for your first assault? You will find answers to all these questions in this book. You will find that often it is only a trick or a knack that makes everything appear so easy when you watch others. After all, even internationally renowned chefs only cook with water.

We will accompany you step for step along your path, from your first simple trials right up to some fancy masterpieces. This book will help you acquire a well grounded basic knowledge of all things edible, will teach you how to decode culinary lingo and

give you the peace of mind to cook in a relaxed manner and have fun doing it. You will be able to dish up meals that will only encourage you to carry on. Well then: Let's get cooking!

In the Beginning was... the Pot

Every aspiring cook should have at his or her disposal a basic array of pots, pans, knives and accessories. These acquisitions might present a little shock to your purse at first, but they are well worth it. Many high-quality kitchen utensils last not only many a year, but a whole lifetime. So you should not be stingy when it comes to buying these things. After all, the wrong pots and pans in which things keep on burning or blunt knives are quite capable of spoiling all the fun. Bear this in mind when going shopping and watch out for quality.

Pots, Pans and Dishes

Pots, frying pans and dishes are especially important articles when it comes to watching out for quality. A proper investment in this category is definitely worth every penny: quality utensils are sturdy and practical. They guarantee short cooking times, which is not only healthy, but also cuts energy costs. Apart from the material itself, details such as a heat conductive, even and thick base, cool-to-the-touch handles and well fitting lids that protect your hands when pouring off boiling water are more important than they might at first appear.

Pots and **frying pans** made out of stainless steel are elegant and practical because you can place them from the stove straight onto the table. Moreover, they are light, easy to clean and always look good. While these are nice side effects, what really matters are their cooking properties and especially the base. A thick base (in the case of stainless steel consisting of multiple layers) is a good conductor of heat and warms the food evenly and without hot spots.

The material used for handles, be it for pots or frying pans, is not that important. Plastic covered handles do not get hot during cooking, enabling

you hold the pot without reverting to oven gloves to do so. However, they usually do not like being put into a hot oven unless they are specifically labelled to be "oven-proof". Stainless steel handles have a special isolating layer between them and the pot, preventing them from becoming as hot as the pot. Again, however, they are do not respond well to being put in a hot oven for any length of time. It is therefore inevitable, that you have to revert back to the good old oven gloves for taking a dish out of the oven. Because this is the first rule in cooking: careful, it is hot! Be it hot liquids, steam, hot plates, spatters of hot fat or hot pots and frying pans, you should always take good care not to hurt yourself or others.

You will also want to take good care when choosing lids. Glass lids are especially useful for the beginner, because you can easily watch what is happening inside the pot without having to lift the lid. This way you do not disturb the cooking process and save energy while you are at it.

We recommend you get a basic set such as the one below, consisting of ten pots:

- 2 casseroles with lids, 6 and 8 inches (16 and 20 cm) diameter
- 2 saucepans with lids, 6 and 7 inches (16 and 18 cm) diameter
- 1 steamer set
- 1 high saucepan, 5 inches (14 cm)
- 1 medium high frying pan with lid, 10 (24 cm) diameters
- 3 bowls, 5, 6 and 8 inches (14, 16 and 20 cm) diameter

Bearing in mind the advantages mentioned above, all your equipment should be made of stainless steal and with the exception of the bowls should have a tight fitting glass lid. Ideal would also be a non-stick coating to avoid burning your food. However, non-stick surfaces are delicate creatures and can easily be scratched.

Using sharp objects such as knives or forks for stirring are therefore out of the question because: a scratched non-stick coating is a no good non-stick coating. You should therefore make sure to use only wooden spoons or plastic utensils. Similarly, you also need to take care during washing up. Never use steel scourers or other abrasive implements, but rinse and wipe the pan with a dish cloth only.

Apart from this basic cooking kit, there are countless special pots and pans which are specifically designed for certain dishes only and not necessary in our everyday kitchen. The "ad-vanced" cook may consider purchasing any number of differently sized **pans**, either stainless steel or non-stick. Depending on your tastes you can extend your collection of cookware in the form of **special pots** or pans to cater for your favourite dishes such as spaghetti or asparagus. Fans of stews or roasts should get a large oval shaped **roasting tin.**

Casserole dishes are especially useful for the beginner. Go out and get some because casseroles are quick and easy to prepare. They cook with a minimum of supervision – all you have to do is put them in the oven – and are served in the same dish. It is therefore advisable that you get yourself 2 or 3 rectangular or oval stainless steel, ceramic or china casserole dishes. Also make sure they come equipped with handles. And once you have the dishes, you will need something to put them on. **Trivets** are not only practical, but also decorative. You can put anything on them ranging from a hot frying pan up to a casserole dish straight out of the oven.

Sieves and Colanders, Knives and Little Kitchen Helpers

Sieves and **colanders**, strainers or filters are needed to drain pasta, rice, potatoes or vegetables. You get sieves with a variety of mesh sizes. The main thing is that they should be functional and easy to clean. Again it will pay if you get yourself good quality gear. Their long life span will outweigh the initial outlay. The ideal utensil is made of stainless steel so that it does not corrode. It must not have sharp edges or recesses. This is not only so that you do not cut yourself but it is also hygienic: no food can get stuck. In any case, one should always rinse utensils with hot water and dry with a dish cloth straight after use.

Knives count among the most important of all kitchen tools. A blunt knife is just about the worst thing that can happen to a cook. Of course, no knife will stay sharp forever – even though some manufacturers' advertisements state just that. Every now and then they do have to be sharpened, but a good quality knife that receives proper care is worth every single penny you spend on it.

Whether large or small, knives should always be made of forged and hardened stainless steel. The blade should extend well into the handle - at least two thirds, more if possible. Moreover, it should be fastened to the handle with two, if not three rivets. The handle should be ergonomically formed and handle well.

A **knife block** for keeping different types of knives not only looks good but is also of great practical value. The blades stay sharp longer because they do not get knocked about so much.

A **sharpening steel** enables you to keep your knives in top condition. The following selection of 6 to 7 knives with different blades and sizes should be sufficient for the beginner:

- 1 cook's knife to cut roasts, sausages, meats and poultry, etc.
- 2 carving knives, one small and one large one to cut fish and meat (including splitting the bone) and to chop herbs
- 1 bread knife with a serrated or scalloped edge
- 2 to 3 small peeling or pairing knives for general kitchen work such as peeling, slicing, cutting, etc.

A variety of **kitchen helpers** are extremely practical and available in all imaginable sizes, shapes, forms and prices. Not all of them may be what you would call useful as some of these contraptions are extremely specialised. However, it is quite possible to develop a fad for them. Kitchen equipment can look rather elegant and present you with an ideal birthday present. Why don't you make it known that you have always wanted a certain kitchen accessory? It certainly is one way of enlarging your kitchen equipment collection. After all, it should keep up with the continuous development of your cooking skills.

For those who like eating vegetables a **peeler** or **swivel peeler** is a nice gadget to call one's own and it really is useful for peeling potatoes and vegetables.

You can cut fruit and vegetables with a knife, but **graters**, **slicers** or **planes** will give the meaning of the word a whole new dimension. A set of solid, sharp, non-slip and easy to clean graters will benefit your kitchen greatly.

Connoisseurs and those aspiring to it should also think about acquiring a small **nutmeg grater**, as ground nutmeg simply cannot compare with the freshly grated variety.

Other everyday kitchen utensils include **multi-purpose kitchen scis-**

sors that should cut through small bones every now and then. Also **wooden spoons** to stir, a **skimmer** to skim off froth and a **kitchen spoon** for basting count among the absolute essentials. You will also find that you will rneed **metal** and **plastic spatulas** – especially useful for stirring and getting the last bits and pieces out of a pot – and a metal **whisk** with well fasted wire loops on a regular basis. Again, good quality does not come cheap, but the long lifespan and toughness of more expensive equipment cannot fail to convince even the most ardent skinflint.

A **meat fork** and a **citrus fruit juicer** are also useful items, although how often you need them will depend on what you cook. Nevertheless, they are part and parcel of a well equipped kitchen.

Pizza fans might well consider purchasing special non-stick **baking trays** and a **pizza cutter** that cuts your pizza quickly and easily.

An electric **hand blender** is easy to handle and even easier to clean. It is an excellent alternative to hand-mixers, normal blenders or even larger kitchen machines.

Tins for storing and keeping foodstuffs fresh exist in all shapes, sizes and colours. The choice is yours, they all do their job.

For those who discover or already know that they simply cannot do without delicious crispy titbits, a **deep fryer** is an absolute essential. What sort of capacity you want your fryer to have depends largely on the number of mouths you have to feed and how many guests you are likely to entertain. Modern deep fryers are technically very advanced and do not differ greatly from one another. They all have permanent odour filters, do not smoke and are very easy to clean.

Kitchen conversion tables

1 tablespoon = 3 teaspoons
1 tablespoon = 1/2 fl oz (10 ml)
1 tablespoon caster sugar = 1/3 oz (10 g)
1 tablespoon sugar = 1/2 oz (15 g)
1 tablespoon breadcrumbs = 1/3 oz (10 g)
1 tablespoon flour = 1/2 oz (15 g)
1 tablespoon butter = 1/2 oz (15 g)

The Know-How

After you have stocked up sufficiently on kitchen equipment you will now get to know some useful things about cooking itself: from flavours and seasonings via quick insights into techniques right up to a guide on what to do in case of an emergency.

The Right Flavour

Herbs and seasonings lend a meal the special touch. Moreover, they are healthy because they contain a variety of vitamins and help to cut down your salt intake. Some herbs or seasonings have healing properties, others just contribute to a general feeling of well-being. Some whet one's appetite and liven up your metabolism while others improve your digestion. And there is more: they add a touch of freshness to the kitchen and a smell of spring and summer, of the Mediterranean or the Far East. Let yourself be inspired!

Specialists still cannot agree on whether a wort can be a herb and a seasoning at the same time. For our purposes, however, it is quite sufficient to note the following: we count as herbs those leaves or leaf-like bits we pluck off smaller plants.

Seasonings consist of dried parts of plants such as leaves, seeds, pods, fruits, roots and stem, etc. from larger bushes or trees.

Whether seasoning or herb, the most important thing is that we approach the matter with some feeling. After all, we do not want the taste of our ingredients or dishes to be overpowered or worse destroyed. Often a pinch of this seasoning or a few leaves of that herb will do just fine. Do not forget: when it comes to seasoning less is often more.

You can grow kitchen herbs on the window sill, the balcony or better still in the garden if you have one. A flowering kitchen herb is an insect's paradise, a pleasure for the senses and an individual and fragrant decoration for the dinner table. To get the best of the aroma you should harvest the leaves prior to flowering.

The following summary introduces the most important kitchen herbs, deals with their flavour and gives some tips which herbs harmonise best with which dishes.

Basil

Basil displays an aromatic peppery taste that also has a sweet quality to it. Those dishes cooked with basil acquire a special Italian touch. It goes best with dishes that include vegetables such as tomatoes, aubergines and peppers, but is not amiss in a fresh summer salad, either.

Savoury

Savoury has a fine peppery note and is simply the herb for all things to do with beans. However, it also lends cabbage, lamb and mushroom dishes as well as salads and casseroles a special touch.

Dill

Dill is a fine wort for fish and seafood, light sauces and veal.

Tarragon

Tarragon has a tart, savoury and rather intense flavour and should therefore be used in small doses. It lends sauces, soups, salads, meat and poultry dishes a unique flavour.

Chervil

Chervil should only be used when fresh because only then will its hearty sweetish flavour liven up you salads, soups, green sauces, herb butter or dips.

Garlic

Garlic is the king of herbs. A member of the leek family, it has a very strong flavour that will add kick to many a dish. One could hardly imagine Southern cuisine without it. You should always use fresh garlic if possible.

Lovage

Nowadays lovage has almost been forgotten. In its heyday it was a firm regular in any cottage garden worth its salt. This aromatic, lovely smelling wort is reminiscent of a well known German kitchen sauce and is now sold mainly in mixed bunches of herbs.

Fresh Coriander

Fresh coriander is an absolute must in the new multi-cultural kitchen. It is available all year round. The spicy, savoury flavour which is reminiscent of aniseed is often used in the Tex-Mex and Asian cuisines.

Marjoram

Marjoram is a classic herb with a tangy, savoury taste that lends foods such as sausages, minced meat, potatoes, liver and roast goose their distinctive flavour. You can use marjoram either fresh or dried, as the latter is only marginally less potent than its fresh counterpart.

Oregano

Oregano is marjoram's Italian cousin. Its savoury flavour provides you with the Italian touch and conjures up little Italy on your plate.

Parsley

Parsley is the most famous of herbs and adds a certain touch of finesse to any dish. The smooth leaves have slightly more flavour than their curly counterparts.

Rosemary

Rosemary is savoury, aromatic and very dominant. Because of this it does not go with other herbs and should be used sparingly. Poultry, venison and lamb benefit especially from rosemary.

Chives

Chives are only used fresh. The taste is reminiscent of onions and, similar to parsley, chives go well with just about any dish. You sprinkle it over your plate just before serving.

Sage

Sage is a natural cure for sore throats. It has a strong flavour that goes well with all veal, lamb, poultry, liver and fish dishes. It has bluish purple flowers.

Thyme

In terms of taste, thyme lies somewhere between savoury and marjoram. The tart, aromatic wort is an integral part of the provencal herb mixture.

Lemon Balm

Lemon balm has a fresh, lemonish taste that goes very well with white meats, fish, salads and desserts.

Seasoning has always been associated with a taste of freedom, adventures and far-away places. These days the spice trade is not a dangerous, let alone adventurous undertaking any more. Fortunately, times have changed since the multi coloured bags containing mysterious powder were worth literally their weight in gold and only the rich and famous could spice up their meals. Nowadays we do not think twice when we encounter goodies from all over the world in our local supermarket, all packed in manageable portions and specially packaged to preserve their aroma. We can take home a touch of the exotic any time we wish, enabling us to cook a great variety of dishes.

It is a true art to season well and make a dish interesting and unusual at the same time. The following paragraphs will tell you all about the most important seasonings and their properties. With this background knowledge you will be able to create any number of aromas:

Cayenne Pepper

Cayenne pepper is a devilishly hot spice that consists of small ground peppers. One should use it sparingly.

Chilli Powder

Chilli powder is a mixture of many ingredients. The above mentioned cayenne pepper forms its basis, but it also contains ground coriander, garlic and ground oregano to round off the taste. Mexican cuisine without chilli powder is quite simply unthinkable and a chilli-con-carne without it would not be the same.

Curry

Curry is a mixture of Asian spices consisting of at least ten different individual flavours including cinnamon, cloves, caraway, curcuma, ginger and pepper. In Asia it is quite normal for each cook to make their own version. In Europe the yellowish brown powder is on offer in varying degrees of hotness.

Ginger

Ginger can be bought either as fresh root ginger or as a ground powder. It has a hot but aromatic taste and lends an Asian touch to all dishes.

Capers

Capers are savoury tangy berries of the Mediterranean caper bush. Some dishes rely on capers for their distinctive flavour and cannot do without.

Caraway

Caraway seeds make pork, cabbage and especially fatty foods more easily digestible. Moreover, its distinctive flavour stamps its authority on many a dish. Caraway is quite similar to garlic – either you really like its distinctive flavour or you absolutely hate it.

Nutmeg

Nutmeg is at its best when freshly grated. The hazelnut sized, very hard, brown silvery nut has an intensive flavour and gives that special touch to poultry and vegetable dishes.

Cloves

Cloves have an aromatic savoury taste and go particularly well with venison and game. They also go well with marinades and stocks, in which they can fully develop their unique taste.

Paprika

Paprika is a more or less hot red powder and the basic seasoning of Hungarian cooking. It consists mainly of red peppers.

Pepper

Pepper, apart from salt, is the universal seasoning par excellence. White pepper is somewhat milder, while black pepper has a stronger taste.

Juniper Berries

Juniper berries have a distinctive gin taste. The strong, wilful aroma goes well with venison and cabbage. The dried brown berries are cooked with the food, but removed prior to serving.

Clever Shopping – the Most Effective Way of Stocking Up Your Larder

Shopping, like cooking, is a lot easier if you are well organised and go about it in a systematic manner. The most important thing you need to do when you go shopping, however, is to have a good meal. For those who enter a supermarket on an empty stomach will grab the first thing in sight and pile their trolley up high with stuff which takes their fancy. In the end you usually have forgotten most of the things you actually went in for.

It is advisable to approach things step by step:
➡ Decide what sort of things you would like to eat over the next few days. Are any visitations on the horizon?
➡ Check your refrigerator and larder to see what you need to stock up on
➡ Check your freezer and refrigerator to see what foods you have to use up quickly. Make space for special offers. Freeze some leftovers which are still good for another meal. Also make sure you have something in the freezer for surprise guests.
➡ Make a shopping list and only head for the supermarket when you have enough time and the aforesaid full stomach.
➡ In between your weekly shopping trips only get stuff like bread, bread rolls, fresh fruit and vegetables. Note that fresh products keep in the refrigerator no longer than a few days.

A well stocked larder is a secret to success. And even in the smallest kitchen there is enough space for a well stocked cupboard. Below you will find a summary of the most important foods you should never be without. If you stick to it, you will always be able to dish up something delicious in no time at all.

Staples
• Salt
• Pepper, black and white
• Sugar, preferably cane sugar
• Flour, palin and brown
• Pasta, rice and potatoes
• Bulgur, couscous, millet, pot barley
• Dried pulses such as lentils, peas and beans have always been considered excellent for keeping fit and offer seemingly endless possibilities. They are rich in protein, carbohydrates, vitamins as well as minerals and fibres
• Vinegars such as red and white wine vinegars, balsamico vinegar and raspberry vinegar
• Oils for salads and for cooking such as sunflower oil, olive oil and chilli, hazelnut or walnut oil depending on your taste

Fresh Foods
• Butter, eggs
• Cheese such as Cheddar or Stilton, grated Cheddar for a pizza or a casserole is readily available and you will save quite a bit of time. Also ideal for freezing.
• Fruit and vegetables – for the small purse it is best not to spend large amounts of money on out-of-season foods, but to eat in accordance with the seasons. Watch out for seasonal special offers!
• Nuts and seeds such as walnuts and hazelnuts both chopped and sliced, sunflower seeds and pumpkin seeds
• Oats

Ready Made Products
• Stocks such as vegetable, beef, poultry and fish stocks
• Vegetable based sauce thickener
• Stock cubes
• Preserved vegetables such as sweetcorn, gherkins, mixed pickles or beetroot, tinned or in a preserving jar
• Tinned fruit such as pineapple, lychees, tangerines and peaches
• Dried herbs such as marjoram, oregano, rosemary and thyme
• Tomato purée

Frozen Products
Frozen products are often cheaper than their fresh counterparts, a good example for this being seafood. Also the quality of frozen products is extremely high. Prior to buying you must check the "best before" date. Also make sure to transport your frozen products in a specially thermally insulated bag – readily available in a well stocked supermarket – in order to avoid spoiling the food.
• Vegetables such as peas, carrots, broccoli and Brussels sprouts
• Herbs such as chives, parsley and herb mixtures such as the 8-herb-mixture or Italian herbs
• Fruit such as raspberries, black currants and blueberries
• Fish such as seafood, fillets of fish and shrimps
• Meat and poultry – can also be bough fresh. This, however, requires stringent planning as it should not be stored for too long a period. Minced meat, for example, should always be used up on the very same day. Frozen products are of a very high quality and can sometimes be stored for months.

The Little A to Z
of Kitchen Lingo

Add liquid:
Adding a little liquid such as stock, water or wine to the frying pan. Careful, it can splatter.

Sauté:
Frying meat on a high flame. This closes the pores and the meat stays nice and juicy.

Blanch:
Simmering vegetables for a short period before holding them under running cold water.

Season:
Seasoning the dish according to your own personal taste. Be careful when you taste the contents of the pot, they are hot!

Fry:
Cooking food in hot fat.

Steam:
Cooking in steam using a special pot with inset or a traditional food steamer.

Rinse:
Pouring cold water over cooked vegetables. This way they keep their colour.

Bind:
Thickening of sauces or soups. Ready-made sauce binders or cornflour, flour, egg yolk, single cream or curdled milk products are ideal for this.

Stew:
Cooking gently in own juice or in just a little bit of liquid on a low flame. Make sure the lid is on.

Marinade:
Putting ingredients into a seasoned, sour liquid to steep. Make sure the bowl is covered. The marinade softens meat, poultry, fish and vegetables, shortens cooking times and also adds a great deal of taste to your dish.

Coat with Breadcrumbs:
Prior to frying or deep frying, turning ingredients first into flour, then beaten eggs and finally in breadcrumbs. This makes for a golden brown, crispy crust while preserving a tender inside.

Braise:
Simmering sautéed foods in liquid on a low flame in a covered pot or on o baking tray in the oven.

In Case of Emergency:

Burnt:
Whatever you do, do not stir! Carefully transfer the food to another pot, taking the utmost care not to disturb the burnt layer at the bottom. Add water and a squirt of washing-up liquid to the burnt pot and bring to the boil. Under no circumstances try to scrape off the burnt food.

Too Much Salt:
Add a little instant mashed potato and cook for couple of minutes. Or take off the heat and add single cream, sour cream or yoghurt.

Too Thin:
Thicken sauce or soup with sauce binder. Do not forget to season again afterwards if necessary

Too Thick:
Thin the soup or sauce with ready-made stock. Add little by little, stirring constantly so as not too make it too thin again.

Tips and Tricks

Aluminium foil is a great all-round helper in the kitchen. You can use it for cooking and grilling, to cover delicate areas during frying and for warming food or keeping it warm. It is also ideal for covering bottles or bowls and gives a tight fit. If you handle good quality foil carefully you can reuse it quite often – it is entirely neutral to different odours.

For safety's sake **eggs** should always be cracked into a cup first and then added to the meal. This way you will recognize a bad egg in time and avoid broken egg shell in your dish.

Fresh mushrooms should be sprinkled with lemon juice immediately after you have sliced them. This keeps them nice and white. The same applies to apples, root celery and avocado pears.

Bunches of herbs or **seasoning** that has to be removed from the pot prior to serving should be tied up in a piece of gauze or placed in a tea ball.

Transfer left-overs from **opened tins** into a different container. Do not keep them longer than a day in the refrigerator.

Pour boiling water over whole **almonds**. This makes them easier to peel.

To peel **tomatoes**, make cross-wise incisions, cover with boiling water and rinse under the running cold tap. This way the skin will come off without a hitch.

Vegetables belonging to the nightshade family such as **tomatoes**, **aubergines** or **peppers** should always have the stem removed because the green bits are poisonous.

Handle cooked **beetroot** with gloves to protect your hands.

It is easy to slice **meat** or **bacon** very thinly if you place it into the freezer for a short time beforehand.

Keep **frozen food** in the proper freezing compartment of your refrigerator. Make sure it has at least three or four stars. Frozen food in a refrigerator with just one star will only keep for one or two days at the most.

Freezing food saves time and you are always prepared for surprise visitors. Be generous when cooking stews, ragouts, goulash or roasts with gravy, pack leftovers into appropriate portions and freeze.

Make a Start...

Salads, snacks and finger food: a small intermezzo in between, crispy fresh summer snacks or tasty bits for the small appetite or the party buffet. Just a little effort can go a long way. We will show you uncomplicated dishes with which you can experiment. Let your creativity get the better of you!

Potato Salad

13 oz (400 g) salad potatoes

1 tsp caraway seeds

1 tbsp coarse salt

1 bunch radish

7 tbsp mayonnaise

1/2 pint (250 ml) buttermilk

1/2 tsp sugar

1 tbsp lemon juice

2 medium sized gherkins

5 oz (150 g) tinned sweetcorn

5 oz (150 g) frozen herb mix

pepper

dill for decoration

Preparation time: approx. 40 minutes
Per serving: approx. 335 cals/1409 kj

1 Wash the potatoes thoroughly and transfer to a pot full of water. Add the caraway seeds and salt and simmer on a low flame for approximately 20 minutes.

2 Wash the radishes and chop the leaves. Slice the radishes. Mix together the mayonnaise and buttermilk in a bowl and stir in the sugar and lemon juice.

3 Drain the gherkins and sweetcorn using a colander. Chop the gherkins. Drain the potatoes and leave to cool. Peel and slice the potatoes and transfer them to a bowl. Add the vegetables.

4 Stir the defrosted herbs into the mayonnaise mixture and season with salt and pepper. Mix together with the salad and leave to steep for approximately 10 minutes. Arrange on plates and decorate with dill.

Different types of potatoes cook differently.
You distinguish between
waxy and fluffy potatoes.
The former are ideally suited for boiling
or potato salad.
Just ask when you go shopping.

Potatoes with Dips

2 lb (900 g) small new potatoes

2 tsp caraway seeds

10 oz (300 g) tomato ketchup

2 tbsp coarse salt,
5 tbsp sour cream,
2 tbsp chilli sauce

salt, pepper,
garlic powder

1 shot Tabasco sauce

5 oz (150 g) beetroot from a jar

7 oz (200 g) cream cheese,
3 tbsp single cream

4 tbsp creamed horseradish,
1 bunch dill, 1/2 tsp sugar

Preparation time: approx. 30 minutes
Per serving: approx. 425 cals/1785 kj

1 Wash the potatoes thoroughly. Use only potatoes that do not have green or rotten black bits. Place them into a pot filled with water.

2 Add the caraway seeds and salt and simmer over a low flame for approximately 20 minutes. In the meantime mix together the sour cream, ketchup and chilli sauce and season with the spices and Tabasco sauce.

3 Drain the beetroot using a colander and dice. Mix together the cream cheese and single cream. Stir in the diced beetroot, creamed horseradish and chopped dill.

4 Season with sugar, salt and pepper. Drain the potatoes and rinse with cold water for easier peeling. Peel the potatoes and serve with the dips.

Sausage Salad

3 gherkins pickled in mustard seeds

1 Spanish onion

10 oz (300 g) pork sausage

7 oz (200 g) tinned or preserved baby corn

1 vegetable stock cube

1/4 pint (125 ml) raspberry vinegar

1/4 pint (125 ml) sunflower oil

1 tsp salt

1/2 tsp pepper

1/2 bunch parsley

Preparation time: approx. 40 minutes
Per serving: approx. 608 cals/2555 kj

1 Drain the gherkins using a colander, then dice them. Peel and dice the onion. Peel and slice the pork sausage, then cut into strips.

2 Drain the baby corn using a colander and cut into chunks. Place in a bowl together with the sausage, onion and gherkins. Heat 1/4 (125 ml) pint water in a pot and dissolve the vegetable stock cube.

3 Mix together the raspberry vinegar and sunflower oil and season with salt and pepper. Add the cool vegetable stock. Wash and dry the parsley. Pluck off a few leaves for decoration, chop the rest into strips and mix it into the stock.

4 Pour the sauce over the salad ingredients, toss and leave to steep for approximately 10 minutes. Arrange on plates and decorate with the left over parsley leaves.

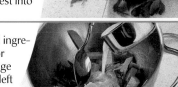

Fresh Pasta Salad

8 oz (250 g) spaghetti

1 tbsp olive oil

3 1/2 oz (100 g) cherry tomatoes

1 yellow pepper

5 oz (150 g) Cheddar

4 celery stalks

Italian herbs (frozen or fresh)

1/4 pint (125 ml) olive oil

4 tbsp fruit vinegar (for example apple vinegar)

salt

pepper

paprika

Preparation time: approx. 35 minutes
Per serving: approx. 631 cals/2651 kj

1 Cook the spaghetti following the instructions on the packet in slightly salted water for approximately 10 minutes. Add a touch of oil so that the pasta does not stick together.

2 In the meantime wash, halve and cut the tomatoes into small slices. Wash, halve and deseed the pepper and cut into thin strips. Cut the cheese into thin strips, too.

3 After about 10 minutes drain the spaghetti and rinse with cold water using a colander. Leave to dry and cool.

4 Wash, dry and slice the celery stalks. Transfer the spaghetti and vegetables into a bowl and mix well. Make up the salad dressing with the olive oil, fruit vinegar and the rest of the herbs.

5 Season well with salt, pepper and paprika. Pour the dressing over the salad ingredients and toss well. Leave to steep for some 10 minutes and arrange on plates.

Shrimp Cocktail

10 oz (300 g) frozen shrimps

1 tbsp lemon juice

5 oz (150 g) lamb's lettuce

7 oz (200 g) tinned tangerines

7 oz (200 g) oyster mushrooms

3 1/2 oz (100 g) mung bean sprouts

10 tbsp curried ketchup

6 tbsp sour cream

2 tbsp olive oil

1/2 tsp salt

1/2 tsp pepper

1/2 tsp paprika powder

4 decorative lollo rosso leaves

Preparation time: approx. 25 minutes
Per serving: approx. 316 cals/1329 kj

1 Wash and drain the shrimps using a colander. Transfer to a bowl and pour over the lemon juice. Wash and dry the lamb's lettuce and remove any limp and yellow leaves.

2 Drain the tangerines using a colander making sure to keep the juice. Wash, dry and slice the oyster mushrooms. Drain the mung bean sprouts using a colander.

3 Transfer the shrimps, tangerines, oyster mushrooms and mung bean sprouts into a bowl and mix carefully. For the dressing mix the ketchup with the sour cream, tangerine juice, olive oil, salt, pepper and paprika.

4 Wash and dry the lollo rosso and arrange together with the lamb's lettuce over the base of small glass bowls. Spoon the shrimp mixture into the bowls and pour over the source.

Why don't you try this refreshing snack with frozen crayfish or king prawns for a change? It adds a sophisticated touch if you serve this cocktail in bread rolls. Just slice two rolls in half, scoop out the dough and arrange the shrimps with sauce in the rolls.

Fitness Salad

2 braeburn or pink lady apples

4 carrots

2 papayas

3 tbsp lemon juice

1 bunch spring onions

2 chicory

10 oz (300 g) cold roast pork

6 tbsp multi-vitamin juice

3 1/2 fl oz (100 ml) sour milk

1/2 bunch parsley

salt

pepper

8 taco wraps

Preparation time: approx. 20 minutes
Per serving: approx. 314 cals/1321 kj

1 Wash, peel and halve the apples. Remove the core and grate into a bowl. Peel the carrots and grate. Halve the papayas and scrape the seeds out with a spoon.

2 First slice the pulp of the papaya and then dice it. Transfer to the bowl together with the apples and carrots and mix. Pour over the lemon juice. Wash and dry the onions and cut into rings.

3 Wash the chicory and remove unsightly leaves. Halve and remove the bitter stump of about 2 inches (4 to 5 cm) in length. Finally slice the chicory into thin strips.

4 Slice the roast pork and add to the other ingredients already in the bowl and toss thoroughly. Also mix together the multi-vitamin juice, sour milk, chopped parsley, salt and pepper.

5 Pour the dressing over the salad and toss well. Transfer the salad into the taco wraps, arrange on plates and serve.

Fillet of White Herring with Sour Cream

4 double fillets of white herring

1 1/4 pints (650 ml) buttermilk

3 eggs, 3 1/2 fl oz (100 ml) vinegar

3 gherkins

3 tbsp capers

3 1/2 oz (100 ml) pickled onions

1/2 bunch parsley

2 oz (50 g) basil

1 tsp hot mustard

12 oz (350 g) sour cream

salt, pepper, garlic powder

4 slices farmhouse bread

3 tbsp butter

*Preparation time: approx. 35 minutes
(plus steeping time)
Per serving: approx. 685 cals/2877 kj*

1 Place the fillets of white herring in a flat bowl and cover with the buttermilk. Leave to steep for approximately 45 minutes. This softens the fish nicely. Boil the eggs for some 8 minutes in water with a touch of vinegar.

2 In the meantime drain the gherkins and capers using a colander. Dice the gherkins. Drain the pickled onions. Wash, dry and chop the herbs.

3 Mix together the mustard, herbs and sour cream and season with the spices. Remove the eggs from the boiling water and rinse under the running cold tap. Peel and halve. Remove the yolk and mash the egg yolks with a fork.

4 Dice the egg whites and add to the sour cream. Add the egg yolks, gherkins, capers and onions. If too thick, add some buttermilk.

5 Remove the fish, drain and cut off the tails. Cut the fillets into bite-sized pieces. Then stir into the egg and sour cream mixture. Season with salt, pepper and garlic powder and arrange on plates. Take the slices of bread, spread butter on them and serve with the fillets of white herring.

Colourful Breast of Duck Carpaccio

13 oz (400 g) smoked breast of duck (get your butcher to slice it very thinly for you)

8 oz (250 g) tinned palm hearts

1 red pepper

5 oz (150 g) tinned Mexican vegetables

8 tbsp olive oil

2 tbsp raspberry vinegar

3 1/2 oz (100 g) frozen Italian herbs

salt

pepper

1 French stick

3 1/2 oz (100 g) herb butter

Preparation time: approx. 20 minutes
Per serving: approx. 672 cals/2825 kj

1 Place the duck breast in a fan like fashion on four plates. Drain the palm hearts using a colander before slicing them thinly.

2 Wash the red pepper and cut in half lengthwise. Deseed and slice. Drain the Mexican vegetable mixture using a colander. Toss together the palm hearts, red pepper and Mexican vegetables.

3 Mix together the olive oil, vinegar and defrosted Italian herbs and season well with salt and pepper. Transfer the vegetables to the four plates and sprinkle with the dressing.

4 Slice and toast the French stick before spreading on the herb butter and serve with the breast of duck carpaccio.

Going Potty!

Soups, stews, pasta and more – these are not just recipes past their prime, dug out from dusty cellars, but are real all time greats. They are simple to prepare, cheap and tasty and make for ideal starters or main courses during any season. These recipes arm you against any surprise visit and are just as suitable for rounding off a cleverly thought through three-course meal.

Broad Bean Stew

2 red onions

2 cloves of garlic

3 tbsp olive oil

3 1/2 oz (100 g) tomato purée

1 tbsp dried thyme

1/2 tbsp dried savoury

1 1/4 lbs (600 g) frozen broad beans

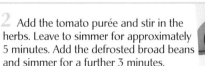

1 pint (600 ml) beef stock

salt, pepper, paprika

4 oz (120 g) Cheddar

Preparation time: approx. 30 minutes
Per serving: approx. 511 cals/2149 kj

1 Peel and cut the onions into rings. Peel the cloves of garlic and crush. Heat the olive oil in a frying pan and sauté the onions and garlic.

2 Add the tomato purée and stir in the herbs. Leave to simmer for approximately 5 minutes. Add the defrosted broad beans and simmer for a further 3 minutes.

3 Add the beef stock and leave to simmer for a further 12 minutes. Season well with salt, pepper and paprika.

4 Grate the cheese using a grater. Transfer the stew onto plates, sprinkle with the grated cheese and serve.

Penne with Spinach

8 oz (250 g) penne rigate

salt

1 tbsp olive oil

2 onions

2 cloves of garlic

3 tbsp olive oil

10 oz (300 g) spinach leaves

5 oz (150 g) ham

1/4 pint (125 ml) single cream

pepper

chilli powder

freshly grated nutmeg

Preparation time: approx. 25 minutes
Per serving: approx. 397 cals/1668 kj

1 Boil the pasta in slightly salted water for approximately 12 minutes. Add the oil so the pasta does not stick together. In the meantime peel and dice the onions.

2 Peel and crush the cloves of garlic. Heat the olive oil in a frying pan and add the onions and garlic. Add the thoroughly washed spinach leaves.

3 Cook the spinach on a low flame for approximately 10 minutes. Cut the ham into strips and together with the single cream stir into the spinach.

4 Season everything with salt, pepper, chilli and a little freshly grated nutmeg. Drain the pasta and transfer to the plates. Pour over the sauce and serve.

Chicken Stew with Rice

1 cooked chicken (approx. 2 lbs)

7 oz (200 g) greens

10 oz (300 g) broccoli

1/2 bunch parsley

1 pint (500 ml) chicken stock

1/2 pint (250 ml) white wine

1/2 root celery

salt

pepper

3 1/2 oz (100 g) 5-minute-rice

Preparation time: approx. 30 minutes
Per serving: approx. 422 cals/1775 kj

1 Place the cooked chicken on your working surface. Take the meat off the bones, remove the skin and cut the meat into small pieces. Wash and cut the greens and broccoli. Chop the parsley.

2 Pour the stock and white wine in a pot and heat on a small flame. Simmer for approximately 15 minutes. Peel and dice the root celery. After 10 minutes cooking time add the greens, vegetables and meat.

3 Leave to simmer for a further 15 minutes and season with salt and pepper. In the meantime cook the rice for some 5 minutes in slightly salted water following the instructions on the packet.

4 Drain the rice and add to the stew. Transfer the stew onto plates, decorate with the chopped parsley and serve.

*A cooked chicken forms the basis of many a meal.
It is ideal for making a quick soup or stew.
Used cold it is ideal for a salad
or in a tasty sandwich.
It is therefore well worth having a chicken at hand.
Deep frozen it will keep a few months and
in the refrigerator a few days
if kept in a closed receptacle.*

...'s Soup

...ef stock to the boil and ...nd herbs. Simmer ...pproximately 15 to ...he soup with salt, ...and ca...seeds.

vegetables

3 1/2 oz (100 g) frozen herb mix

salt

pepper

1/2 tsp caraway seeds

2 onions

2 cloves of garlic

13 oz (400 g) mixed minced meat

1 tbsp breadcrumbs

1 tbsp mustard

cayenne pepper

paprika

1 French stick

Preparation time: approx. 25 minutes
Per serving: approx. 376 cals/1579 kj

2 In the meantime peel and dice the onions. Peel and crush the cloves of garlic. Mix both onions and garlic with the minced meat and add breadcrumbs and mustard. Season the mixture well with salt, pepper and paprika.

3 Wet your hands and take a dab of the meat mixture. Form into little balls.

4 Add the meat balls 5 or 10 minutes before the soup is ready. Slice the French stick. Transfer the soup onto plates and serve with the French stick.

A beefy, nourishing soup continues to be the pride of every good cook. However, the vegetables should remain crisp and tasty and not become mushy or mousse-like because they have been cooked for too long.

Gnocchi with Tomato Sauce

2 oz (50 g) herb butter

1 lb (500 g) tomato purée

3 1/2 oz (100 g) fresh or frozen Italian herb mixture

7 oz (200 g) sour cream

1 fl oz (100 ml) red wine

salt, pepper

1 1/2 lbs (700 g) gnocchi from the refrigerator

1 oz (20 g) butter

hyssop (vervain) and lovage for decoration

Preparation time: approx. 20 minutes
Per serving: approx. 912 cals/3833 kj

1 Melt the herb butter in a pot. Add the tomato purée and mixed herbs. Simmer everything for approximately 2 minutes.

2 Add the sour cream and red wine and heat for 2 minutes stirring continuously. Do not let it come to the boil. Season the tomato sauce with salt and pepper.

3 Cook the gnocchi in slightly salted water following the instructions on the packet. Drain thoroughly using a colander.

4 Melt the butter in a frying pan and fry a handful of gnocchi at a time. Arrange on plates, pour over the sauce and decorate with herbs prior to serving.

Pumpkin Lentil Risotto

3 1/2 oz (100 g) 5-minute-rice

salt

1/2 courgette

1/2 pint vegetable stock

1 yellow pepper

3 1/2 oz (100 g) red lentils

5 oz (150 g) pickled pumpkin

sweet sour

pepper

ground garlic

lemon balm for decoration

Preparation time: approx. 35 minutes
Per serving: approx. 228 cals/960 kj

1 Cook the rice in slightly salted water following the instructions on the packet. In the meantime wash, dry and cut the courgette into small pieces. Bring the stock to the boil.

2 Wash the pepper and cut lengthwise. Deseed and dice the pepper. Add the vegetables together with the lentils to the stock and cook on a low flame for approximately 12 to 15 minutes.

3 Put the pumpkin into a sieve, leave to drain and dice. Add to the vegetables, heat and season with salt and pepper.

4 Wash and dry the lemon balm. Add the rice to the vegetables, mix and put on the heat. Season with garlic, arrange on plates and decorate with the lemon balm.

Spicy Goulash Soup

2 onions

12 oz (350 g) beef goulash

2 cloves of garlic

2 oz (50 g) clarified butter

1 lb (500 g) peeled tomatoes

1/2 pint (250 ml) red wine

2 red peppers

2 red chilli peppers

1 pint (500 ml) beef stock

paprika

salt

pepper

2 to 3 tbsp sour cream

parsley for decoration

Preparation time: approx. 30 minutes
Per serving: approx. 626 cals/2632 kj

1 Peel and dice the onions. Melt the clarified butter and sauté the onions together with the meat and the already peeled and crushed garlic. Add the tomatoes with their juice and the wine.

2 Leave to simmer for approximately 45 minutes. Wash the red peppers and chilli peppers. Cut in half lengthwise and deseed.

3 Finely dice both peppers and chilli peppers and add to the tomato mixture. Cook on a low flame for another 3 to 4 minutes.

4 Add the stock and heat for 2 to 3 minutes, stirring continuously. Season the soup with the spices, making sure it is quite hot. Transfer onto plates, add a spoonful of sour cream and decorate with parsley prior to serving.

Leipzig Pasta Soup

2 to 3 pints (1 to 1 1/2 l) chicken stock

1/4 pint (125 ml) white wine

1 bunch parsley

1 1/4 lbs (600 g) mixed frozen vegetables

1/2 grilled chicken

7 oz (200 g) ready made crayfish meat

3 1/2 oz (100 g) soup pasta

salt, pepper

freshly grated nutmeg

7 oz (200 g) sour cream

Preparation time: approx. 30 minutes
Per serving: approx. 617 cals/2594 kj

1 Bring the chicken stock and the white wine to the boil. Wash, dry and finely chop the parsley. Cook together with the vegetables for approximately 12 minutes on a low heat.

2 In the meantime, halve the grilled chicken and take the meat off the bone. Remove the skin and cut the meat into small pieces. Do the same for the crayfish meat.

3 Add the soup pasta 5 minutes before the soup is ready. Add the chicken and crayfish meat and cook for a further 2 to 3 minutes.

4 Season the soup with salt, pepper and freshly grated nutmeg and transfer onto the plates. Decorate with a spoonful of sour cream and serve.

Brussels Sprouts Beef Stew

2 pints (1 l) beef stock

1/4 pint (125 ml) real ale

3 1/2 oz (100 g) greens

1 1/4 lbs (600 g) Brussels sprouts

1 tbsp tomato purée

1/4 bunch thyme and oregano

salt, pepper

8 oz (250 g) corned beef

Preparation time: approx. 35 minutes
Per serving: approx. 187 cals/787 kj

1 Pour the stock and ale into a pot and bring to the boil. Wash the greens and Brussels sprouts. Chop the greens and add the vegetables and tomato purée to the stock.

2 Simmer on a low flame for approximately 20 minutes. In the meantime wash, dry and chop the herbs and add to the soup. Season with salt and pepper.

3 Crumble the corned beef with a fork and add to the soup shortly before it is ready. Heat everything stirring continuously. Transfer onto plates and serve.

Down the Frying Pan!

Meat, poultry, fish and seafood – it all sounds like a real challenge to the inexperienced cook. However, it is really quite simple. Less and less simple recipes lead the path to the ever diversifying world of fish and meats: we accompany you on the way from such kitchen classics like pork escalopes and lamb curry right down to more elaborate dishes such as steaks and delicate fillets of fish. You will end up being surprised at what are you capable of dishing up!

Scrambled Eggs with Chanterelles

7 oz (200 g) chanterelle
mushrooms

2 oz (50 g) parsley

7 oz (200 g) bacon

3 tomatoes

8 eggs

2 tbsp sparkling mineral water

3 tbsp milk

salt

pepper

4 slices farmhouse bread

2 tbsp butter

Preparation time: approx. 25 minutes
Per serving: approx. 353 cals/1483 kj

1 Clean the chanterelle mushrooms.
Wash, dry and finely chop the parsley.
Slice the rashers of bacon. Sauté in a frying
pan and add the chanterelle mushrooms.

2 Add the parsley after 12 minutes and
leave to steep on a low flame for approximately 3 minutes. In the meantime
wash, halve and slice the tomatoes
and put to one side.

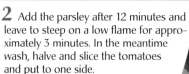

Mushrooms

3 Crack the eggs into a bowl and beat together with the mineral water and milk. Give the mixture a good whisk and season well with salt and pepper.

4 Add the egg mixture to the bacon in the frying pan and leave just long enough to set. Use a fish slice to carefully turn over. Spread the butter on the bread slices and arrange the scrambled eggs on top. Decorate with the slices of tomatoes and serve.

You can use a multitude of ingredients with scrambled eggs and always end up with varied and quickly prepared dishes. For frying it is best to use non-stick coated frying pans – you not only save the extra fat but this will also prevent the egg from burning.

Rissoles on Beans

2 lbs (800 g) mixed minced meat

2 onions

2 cloves of garlic

salt, pepper

paprika and chilli powder

4 tbsp breadcrumbs

1 tbsp hot mustard

3 tbsp tomato purée

1 1/4 lb (600 g) tinned chilli beans

4 tbsp clarified butter

1 bunch basil

2 tbsp herb butter

3 1/2 oz (100 g) tomato purée

Preparation time: approx. 25 minutes
Per serving: approx. 1043 cals/4383 kj

1 Transfer the minced meat into a bowl. Peel and dice the onions. Peel the cloves of garlic and crush with a garlic crusher. Mix the onions and garlic with the meat and season with salt, pepper, paprika and chilli powder.

2 Add the breadcrumbs, mustard and the tomato purée to the meat and knead the mixture. Wet your hands, take a handful of meat and form rissoles. Drain the beans using a colander.

3 Melt the clarified butter in a frying pan and fry the rissoles for approximately 10 minutes. Wash, dry and cut the basil leaves into strips. Melt the herb butter and sauté the beans.

4 Add the tomato purée and basil and leave on a low flame for about 6 minutes. Season with salt, pepper and paprika. Arrange on plates and serve. A French stick makes for an ideal accompaniment.

Hungarian Goulash

1 lb (500 g) Spanish onions

2 cloves of garlic

2 lbs (1 kg) goulash

pepper, paprika

salt

4 tbsp clarified butter

1 pint (500 ml) beef stock

2 red peppers

1/2 pint (250 ml) red wine

4 tbsp crème fraîche

Preparation time: approx. 60 minutes
Per serving: approx. 702 cals/2949 kj

1 Peel and dice the onions. Peel the cloves of garlic and crush. Wash and dry the meat. Melt the clarified butter in a frying pan and sauté the onions in it.

2 Add the meat and the garlic. Use the spices to season well. Add the stock and red wine after about 6 minutes and leave to simmer on a low heat for approximately 40 minutes.

3 In the meantime, wash the red peppers and cut in half lengthwise. Deseed and slice.

4 Add the peppers to the goulash after a good 30 minutes. Shortly before serving stir in the crème fraîche.

5 Season the goulash once more with salt, pepper and paprika. Transfer onto plates and serve with pasta. Penne rigate go particularly well with this dish.

Italian Poultry Rolls

**8 thin turkey escalopes
(3 1/2 oz/100 g each)**

3 1/2 oz (100 g) tomato purée

salt

pepper

8 slices Parma ham

2 onions

1 bunch basil

3 tbsp garlic butter

1 clove of garlic

5 tbsp olive oil

1/4 pint (125 ml) chicken stock

2 fl oz (50 ml) dry sherry

**10 oz (300 g) frozen gourmet
vegetables**

Preparation time: approx. 45 minutes
Per serving: approx. 561 cals/2356 kj

1 Wash and dry the meat. Transfer it onto your working surface. Spread some tomato purée onto each escalope and season with salt and pepper. Place a slice Parma ham on top.

2 Peel and cut the onions into rings. Wash, dry and cut the basil leaves into strips. Melt the butter in a frying pan and sauté the onions, crushed garlic and basil.

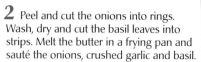

3 Spread the mixture finely onto the escalopes. Roll up the meat and secure with a wooden toothpick. Heat the olive oil in a frying pan and brown the turkey rolls for about 6 minutes on all sides.

4 Add the stock, dry sherry and the defrosted vegetables and leave to simmer on a low flame for approximately 12 minutes. Arrange everything on plates and serve. Brown rice makes for an ideal accompaniment to this dish.

*Poultry has many advantages.
The meat is lean and does not have many calories.
However, it has plenty of proteins and
does not lack taste.
Turkey is quite odd in that every part tastes different.
The white meat from the breast for our rolls
is very tender and delicate.*

Quick Gyros in the Pan

1 1/4 lbs (600 g) pork escalopes

3 tbsp gyros seasoning

3 tbsp olive oil

1 cucumber

2 onions

1 clove of garlic

1 bunch dill

1 tbsp lemon juice

10 oz (300 g) yoghurt

salt

pepper

chilli powder

dill for decoration

*Preparation time: approx. 30 minutes
(plus marinating time)
Per serving: approx. 451 cals/1896 kj*

1 Wash, dry and slice the meat into strips. Season with the gyros seasoning and sprinkle with the olive oil. Mix everything together in a bowl and leave for the marinade to develop its flavour for approximately 45 minutes.

2 In the meantime halve the cucumber lengthwise and deseed by scooping out the seeds with a spoon. Slice the cucumber. Peel and dice the onions. Peel and crush the clove of garlic.

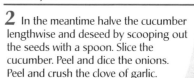

3 Wash, dry and finely chop the dill. Mix together with the cucumber, onions and garlic and sprinkle the lemon juice on top. Add the yoghurt and season well with salt, pepper and chilli powder.

The thinner you slice the pork escalopes the less time it takes to cook. One should always use a high flame to brown the meat in order to close the pores straight away. This ensures that the meat stays nice and juicy. To cook it, however, use a low flame.

4 Brown the meat on all sides without adding fat to the pan and leave to cook for approximately 10 minutes. Arrange on plates and place the cucumber dip next to it. Decorate with the dill and serve. Rice makes for an ideal accompaniment to this dish.

Lamb Curry

1 1/2 lbs (750 g) fillet of lamb

salt

pepper

1 leek stalk

2 carrots

7 oz (200 g) oyster mushrooms

3 tbsp garlic butter

2 tbsp curry powder

1/2 pint (250 ml) vegetable stock

10 oz (280 g) tinned tangerines

3 tbsp sour cream

1/2 bunch coriander

Preparation time: approx. 35 minutes
Per serving: approx. 420 cals/1764 kj

1 Wash, dry and dice the meat and season with salt and pepper. Wash and dry the leek and cut into rings.

2 Wash, peel and slice the carrots. Wash, dry and slice the oyster mushrooms.

3 Melt the butter in a pan and brown the meat for approximately 6 minutes on all sides. Add the vegetables and season with the curry powder. Leave to simmer on a low flame for about 5 minutes.

4 Add the vegetable stock and leave to simmer for a further 10 minutes. Drain the tangerines using a sieve and add to the meat 2 minutes prior to serving the dish.

5 Add the sour cream and season once again with the spices and seasonings. Wash, dry and rip the leaves off the coriander and use them for decorating. Brown rice makes for an ideal accompaniment.

Chicken Liver with Sage

1 1/2 lbs (650 g) chicken liver

1 tbsp flour

1 onion

1 clove of garlic

3 tbsp clarified butter

salt

pepper

1/2 bunch sage

Preparation time: approx. 20 minutes
Per serving: approx. 651 cals/2735 kj

1 Wash, dry and sprinkle the flour on the liver. Peel and dice the onion. Peel the clove of garlic and crush using a garlic crusher.

2 Melt the clarified butter in a frying pan and sauté the onion. Add the meat and the crushed garlic and season well with salt and pepper.

3 Wash and dry the sage. Pluck the leaves off the stems and cut into strips. Add to the meat and cook on a low flame for approximately 5 minutes. Arrange on plates and serve with mashed potatoes.

Tasty Pork Cutlets

4 pork cutlets (7 oz/200g each)

salt

pepper

3 tbsp clarified butter

1/2 pint (250 ml) red wine

7 oz (200 g) pickled onions

5 oz (150 g) sour cream

1 bunch parsley

Preparation time: approx. 20 minutes
Per serving: approx. 593 cals/2490 kj

1 Wash and dry the meat and season with salt and pepper. Score the edge with a sharp knife so that they do not arch during cooking and deform the cutlets.

2 Melt the clarified butter and brown the meat on each side for approximately 3 minutes before adding the wine. Leave to simmer on a low heat for about 6 minutes, turning the cutlets every now and then.

3 Remove the cutlets and keep warm. Drain the pickled onions in a sieve and add to the frying pan. Bring to the boil and add the sour cream.

4 Wash, dry and cut the parsley into strips. Add to the sauce. Season with salt and pepper. Arrange the cutlets on the plates and pour over the sauce. Serve with pasta.

Salmon Steaks with Fennel

4 salmon steaks (including skin and bone)

1 tbsp lemon juice

3 tbsp herb butter

salt

pepper

3 fennel bulbs

1/2 (250 ml) pint white wine

7 oz (200 g) crème fraîche

1 tbsp sweet mustard

Preparation time: approx. 30 minutes
Per serving: approx. 708 cals/2973 kj

1 Wash and dry the salmon. Sprinkle the lemon juice over the fish. Melt the herb butter in a frying pan and brown the salmon on both sides for approximately 5 minutes. Season with salt and pepper.

2 Remove the salmon and wrap in aluminium foil. Keep warm. Wash and dry the fennel and cut into thin strips. Put aside the green leaves for decoration purposes.

3 Reheat the contents of the frying pan and sauté the fennel. Add the white wine after approximately 3 minutes and leave to simmer on a low flame for another 3 minutes.

4 Mix the crème fraîche with the sweet mustard and add to the vegetables. Arrange the salmon steaks on the plates and add the fennel. Decorate with the fennel green and serve with boiled potatoes.

Fish is very healthy and can be cooked in many different variations. Many kinds of fish, especially salmon, are available fresh throughout the year and are of excellent quality. Regardless of whether you buy it fresh or frozen, always transport it in a special insulated bag. Fresh fish should be consumed the same day you bought it.

Cordon Bleu

4 slices shoulder of pork (have your butcher make a pocket like incision in each slice)

4 slices ham

10 oz (300 g) Stilton

3 tbsp sweet mustard

salt

pepper

ground caraway

3 tbsp clarified butter

Preparation time: approx. 25 minutes
Per serving: approx. 723 cals/3037 kj

1 Wash and dry the shoulder of pork. Transfer the ham slices on your working surface. Slice the cheese and place on top of the ham.

2 Fold the ham slices in such a way to wrap the cheese in them and place into the pockets of the shoulder of pork. Fasten the opening with a wooden toothpick. Cover the pork with mustard and season with salt, pepper and the ground caraway.

3 Melt the clarified butter in a frying pan and brown the meat on a high flame for approximately 3 minutes on each side. Then reduce the heat and fry the pork for about 10 minutes on a low flame with a closed lid. Arrange on plates and serve with potato salad.

Fillet of Dover Sole in Grape Sauce

1 1/4 lbs (600 g) frozen fillets of
Dover sole

1 tbsp lemon juice

4 tbsp olive oil

salt

pepper

8 oz (250 g) black grapes

6 fl oz (180 ml) fish
stock

2 tbsp pickled green
peppercorns

1 fl oz (2 cl) brandy

7 oz (200 g) sour cream

Preparation time: approx. 25 minutes
Per serving: approx. 413 cals/1736 kj

1 Defrost the fish, wash, dry and
sprinkle with the lemon juice. Heat the
olive oil in a frying pan and brown the
fish from both sides for approximately
4 minutes. Season with salt and pepper.

2 Wrap the fillets in aluminium foil and
keep warm. Wash and dry the grapes
before slicing them in half and deseeding
them. Heat up the contents of the frying
pan and sauté the grapes.

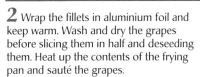

3 Add the fish stock to the grapes. Drain
the pickled green peppercorns using a
sieve and add together with the brandy.
Leave to simmer on a low heat for approximately 3 minutes.

4 Shortly before serving stir in the sour
cream and season with salt and pepper.
Arrange the fish on plates and pour over
the sauce. A French stick makes for an
ideal accompaniment to this dish.

Pork Escalopes

**4 pork escalopes (5 oz/
150 g each)**

salt

pepper

butter

13 oz (400 g) tomatoes

1 onion

2 cloves of garlic

2 tbsp raspberry vinegar

1 tsp sugar

3 tbsp double cream

herbs for decoration

*Preparation time: approx. 25 minutes
Per serving: approx. 348 cals/ 1461 kj*

1 Wash and dry the meat and season with salt and pepper. Melt the butter in a frying pan and brown the meat on both sides for approximately 6 minutes.

2 Wrap the meat in aluminium foil and keep warm. Wash, half and slice the tomatoes. Peel and dice the onions. Peel the cloves of garlic and crush.

3 Reheat the contents of the frying pan and sauté the vegetables. Add the raspberry vinegar and sugar and season with salt and pepper. Leave to simmer on a low flame for approximately 5 minutes.

4 Add the double cream prior to serving. Arrange the meat on plates, decorate with the herbs and serve with fried potatoes.

*You should try the famous Hungarian
or paprika pork escalopes as well.
You season the meat with salt and pepper,
sprinkle over some lemon juice and fry it in oil.
The accompanying sauce is similar,
consisting of cream and peppers.*

Fillet of Pollock with Vegetables

1 1/2 lbs (700 g) carrots

2 onions

1 tbsp herb butter

1/4 pint (125 ml) vegetable stock

salt

pepper

freshly grated nutmeg

2 tbsp sour cream

4 fillets of pollock (7 oz/200 g each)

1 tbsp lemon juice

2 eggs

3 1/2 oz (100 ml) flour

3 1/2 oz (100 ml) breadcrumbs

5 tbsp clarified butter

Preparation time: approx. 30 minutes
Per serving: approx. 574 cals/2411 kj

1 Wash, peel and slice the carrots. Peel and dice the onions. Melt the herb butter in a frying pan and sauté both carrots and onions.

2 Add the vegetable stock and leave to simmer on a low heat for approximately 10 minutes. Season with salt, pepper and freshly grated nutmeg. Then stir in the sour cream.

3 Wash and dry the fish and sprinkle with the lemon juice. Season with salt and pepper. Beat the eggs and transfer onto a plate. Prepare two other plates, one with the flour and one with the breadcrumbs.

The breadcrumbs prevent the delicate fish fillet (and white and light meats such as poultry and pork) from becoming too dry during frying. Especially children like fish best if fried in breadcrumbs. You should follow the steps outlined above to the letter so as to ensure a nice coating.

4 First cover the fillets in flour and then dip them into the egg mixture. Finally cover them with breadcrumbs. Make sure that the breadcrumbs stick properly so that they do not come off so easily in the frying pan. Melt the clarified butter in a frying pan and fry the fillets for approximately 8 to 10 minutes, turning the fish every now and then. Arrange on plates, add the vegetables and serve with green fettuccine.

Steaks with Sherry Sauce

4 beef steaks (5 oz/150 g each)

2 onions

2 cloves of garlic

3 tbsp olive oil

salt

pepper

1/4 pint (125 ml) beef stock

1/4 pint (125 ml) dry sherry

1 tbsp creamed horseradish

2 tbsp apple juice

Preparation time: approx. 30 minutes
Per serving: approx. 340 cals/1428 kj

1 Wash and dry the meat. Peel and dice the onions. Peel and crush the cloves of garlic using a garlic crusher.

2 Heat the olive oil in a frying pan and brown the meat on both sides for approximately 1 minute on a high heat. Reduce the heat and add the onions and garlic. Season with salt and pepper.

3 After about 3 minutes remove the meat, wrap in aluminium foil and keep warm. Reheat the contents of the frying pan and add the beef stock. Stir in the sherry and creamed horseradish.

4 Leave to simmer on a low flame for approximately 5 minutes. Add the apple juice prior to serving. Arrange the meat on plates, pour on the sauce and serve with croquettes.

The steak is the prime cut of beef. Whether your steaks will be a success depends on the quality of the meat and the frying time. As a rule of thumb: fry a 7 oz/200 g of steak for 1 minute to have very rare and bloody steaks – nearly raw 3 minutes to have rare and bloody steaks – inside nearly raw 4 minutes to have medium steaks – inside nearly cooked 6 minutes to have well done steaks – inside well cooked

Lamb with Herb Crusts

1 lb (500 g) fillet of lamb

2 eggs

3 1/2 oz (100 g) frozen herbs Provencale

3 1/2 oz (100 g) breadcrumbs

3 tbsp clarified butter, 3 tbsp flour

salt, pepper, herbs for decoration

Preparation time: approx. 25 minutes
Per serving: approx. 485 cals/2034 kj

1 Wash, dry and cut the meat into strips. Season with salt and pepper. Break the eggs into a bowl and lightly beat them. Defrost the herbs and mix together with the breadcrumbs.

2 Prepare one plate with the flour and another with the breadcrumbs. Cover the meat with flour, then dip it into the eggs and finally cover it with the breadcrumbs. Make sure they stick properly so as not to come off in the frying pan.

3 Melt the clarified butter in a frying pan and brown the fillets on each side for approximately 4 minutes. Arrange on plates and serve with jacket potatoes with a touch of sour cream.

Tipsy Fillet of Pork

1 1/4 lbs (600 g) ___ ___

2 tbsp clarified ___

salt

pepper

13 oz (400 g) preserved morello cherries

3 tbsp apricot jam

2 fl oz (50 ml) apricot juice

1/4 pint (150 ml) kirsch

7 oz (200 g) sour cream

lemon balm for decoration

Preparation time: approx. 25 minutes
Per serving: approx. 627 cals/2635 kj

1 Wash, dry and slice the fillet of pork. Melt the cl___ ___ ___an ___ ___ for ___ le.

2 Re___ ___ flame and continue to fry the po___ another 6 minutes. Season with salt and pepper. Remove the meat and wrap in aluminium foil. Keep warm. Drain the morello cherries using a sieve.

3 Reheat the contents of the frying pan and sauté the cherries. Stir in the apricot jam and add the meat. Stir in the apricot juice and sprinkle on the Kirsch.

4 Light the alcohol with an extra long match and leave until the flames die down. Stir in the sour cream. Arrange on plates and decorate with the lemon balm. Fried courgettes make for an ideal accompaniment to this dish.

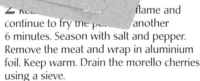

Just Ovenly!

The oven is the core of each and every kitchen. It is at the centre of all things culinary. Vegetables, cheese, meat and fish: almost all ingredients can be combined at will to create a new tasty dish. Prepared without stress and put into the oven these dishes leave you enough time to set the table, have a small aperitif and do whatever else you think belongs to an enjoyable evening.

Exotic Sweet Lasagne

3 bananas, 3 kiwis, 2 mangos

1/2 pineapple

1 lb (500 g) cream cheese

2 tbsp cane sugar

5 tbsp white rum

1/2 tsp ground cinnamon

1/2 tsp ground cardamom

butter to grease the oven-proof dish

8 lasagne sheets

7 oz (200 g) instant custard

4 tbsp desiccated coconut

Preparation time: approx. 25 minutes
Per serving: approx. 516 cals/2169 kj

1 Preheat the oven to gas mark 4 (350° F or 180° C). Peel the fruit, remove the mango stones and cut everything into strips before dicing it.

2 Mix together the cream cheese, cane sugar and white rum. Stir in the fruit and season with the ground cardamom and cinnamon.

3 Grease an oven-proof dish. Place a layer of lasagne sheets in the dish and cover with the cheese mixture. Repeat the process for all the ingredients. Prepare the custard following the instructions on the packet.

4 Stir in the desiccated coconut and spread the sauce over the lasagne. Place in the centre of the oven and bake for approximately 20 minutes. Arrange on plates and serve.

Spicy Baked Potatoes

2 lbs (1 kg) baking potatoes

1/2 tsp caraway seeds

3 tbsp olive oil

8 oz (250 g) mushrooms

3 1/2 oz (100 g) stoned black olives

8 oz (250 g) cherry tomatoes

1 dried chilli pepper

salt, pepper

1 bunch basil

4 tbsp walnut oil

Preparation time: approx. 45 minutes
Per serving: approx. 477 cals/2003 kj

1 Wash the potatoes and cook in slightly salted water with the caraway seeds for approximately 20 minutes. Cover a baking tray with the olive oil and preheat the oven to gas mark 4 (350° F or 180° C).

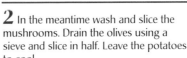

2 In the meantime wash and slice the mushrooms. Drain the olives using a sieve and slice in half. Leave the potatoes to cool.

3 Wash and slice the tomatoes in half. Cut the potatoes into bite sized pieces. Mix the ingredients together with the potatoes and spread onto the baking tray. Crumble the dried chilli pepper and sprinkle over the vegetables. Season with salt and pepper.

4 Wash and dry the basil. Pluck the leaves and cut into strips. Spread over the baking tray. Sprinkle the walnut oil over the ingredients and put in the centre of the oven. Bake for approximately 20 minutes, turning the food every now and then. Arrange on plates and serve with a fresh colourful salad.

Tasty Egg Bake

1 lb (500 g) broccoli

3 tbsp herb butter

salt

pepper

freshly grated nutmeg

3 1/2 oz (100 g) chopped almonds

8 eggs

1/4 pint (125 ml) milk

3 tbsp mineral water

butter to grease the oven-proof dish

4 smoked trout fillets

3 tbsp crème fraîche

5 tbsp creamed horseradish

Preparation time: approx. 30 minutes
Per serving: approx. 751 cals/3156 kj

1 Preheat the oven to gas mark 4 (350° F or 180° C). Wash and separate the broccoli into florets. Melt the butter in a frying pan, sauté the broccoli and season with salt and pepper.

2 Add the chopped almonds and fry for a further 3 minutes. In the meantime mix together the eggs, milk and mineral water in a bowl and season with salt, pepper and freshly grated nutmeg.

3 Grease an oven-proof dish with the butter and fill with the broccoli and egg mixture. Place in the centre of the oven and bake for approximately 18 minutes. When finished, slice and transfer onto four plates.

4 Place a trout fillet on the bake. Mix together the crème fraîche and creamed horseradish and place a spoonful on each plate. Serve with toasted wholemeal bread.

This or a similar kind of egg bake or giant omelette is ideal as a main dish or a party snack. It all depends on how big a portion you serve. Baked eggs in contrast to fried eggs set well and are quite firm so that you can cut it easily.

Vegetable Cheese Gratin

1 1/4 lbs (600 g) frozen ratatouille

3 1/2 oz (100 g) pepper butter

salt, pepper

4 tbsp red wine

butter to grease the oven-proof dish

8 oz (250 g) smoked breast of turkey

7 oz (200 g) Roquefort

Preparation time: approx. 30 minutes
Per serving: approx. 496 cals/2083 kj

1 Defrost the vegetables. Preheat the oven to gas mark 4 (350° F or 180° C). Melt the pepper butter in a frying pan and sauté the vegetables. Season with salt and pepper.

2 Add the red wine and continue to cook for another 2 minutes, stirring constantly. Grease the oven-proof dish with the butter. Transfer the vegetables to the oven-proof dish layer for layer.

3 Cut the smoked breast of turkey into strips and spread over the vegetables. Slice the cheese, too, and transfer to the oven-proof dish. Place the dish in the centre of the oven and bake for approximately 10 minutes.

Seafood Gratin

1 1/2 lbs (750 g) frozen seafood

2 tbsp chilli oil

2 tbsp olive oil

salt, pepper

butter to grease the oven-proof dish

4 tbsp Fernet Branca or other bitter

2 oz (50 g) grated Parmesan cheese

1 oz (30 g) breadcrumbs

1 tsp rosemary, 1 tsp sage

3 tbsp sunflower oil

rosemary for decoration

Preparation time: approx. 30 minutes
Per serving: approx. 496 cals/2083 kj

1 Defrost the seafood following the instructions on the packet. Heat the chilli oil and olive oil in a frying pan and sauté the seafood.

2 Season with salt and pepper and leave on a low flame for approximately 4 minutes. Preheat the oven to gas mark 4 (350° F or 180° C). Grease an oven-proof dish with the butter.

3 Transfer the seafood to the oven-proof dish and sprinkle over the Fernet Branca. Mix together the Parmesan, breadcrumbs, herbs and sunflower oil.

4 Cover the seafood with the mixture and place in the centre of the oven. Bake for approximately 6 minutes or until golden brown. Decorate with rosemary and serve.

Exotic Leg of Chicken

4 chicken legs

salt, pepper

ground ginger and ground garlic

3 tbsp clarified butter

butter to grease the oven-proof dish

1 fl oz (2 cl) sherry

7 oz (200 g) pickled ginger, sweet sour

1 avocado pear, 1/4 pint (125 ml) chicken stock

2 tbsp orange juice

5 oz (150 g) sour cream

some coriander leaves

Preparation time: approx. 40 minutes
Per serving: approx. 949 cals/3987 kj

1 Wash, dry and season the chicken legs with the seasonings. Melt the clarified butter in a frying pan and brown the legs on both sides for approximately 4 minutes. Preheat the oven to gas mark 4 (350° F or 180° C).

2 Grease an oven-proof dish with the butter and place the chicken legs inside. Add the sherry. Place in the centre of the oven and bake for approximately 30 minutes. Baste every now and then with the sherry.

3 In the meantime drain the ginger using a sieve, making sure to catch the liquid. Cut into small pieces. Peel and halve the avocado pear, remove the stone and cut into strips.

4 Reheat the contents of the pan and sauté the ginger. Add the chicken stock, orange juice and the liquid from the pickled ginger. Simmer on a low heat for about 5 minutes. Add the avocado and season with salt, pepper and ground garlic. Stir in the sour cream. Arrange the chicken legs on plates, add the sauce, decorate with the coriander leaves and serve with rice.

Roast Beef with Herbs

2 lbs (1 kg) roast beef

3 tbsp mustard

3 1/2 oz (100 g) frozen herb mixture

2 onions

2 cloves of garlic

2 tbsp olive oil

3 tbsp breadcrumbs

2 tbsp red wine

salt

pepper

Preparation time: approx. 20 minutes (plus baking time)
Per serving: approx. 554 cals/2327 kj

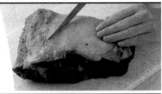

1 Wash and dry the beef. Score the fat with a sharp knife making criss-cross cuts. Preheat the oven to gas mark 8 (450° F or 225° C). Mix together the mustard and herbs.

2 Peel and finely chop the onions. Peel and crush the cloves of garlic. Add both onions and garlic to the mustard mixture. Stir in the breadcrumbs, olive oil and wine and season with salt and pepper.

3 Place the meat fat down into a roasting tin lined with grease proof paper and smother the side facing you with the mustard mixture. Place in the oven and bake for approximately 50 minutes.

4 When the time is up take the meat out of the oven and leave to rest for approximately 10 minutes so as to make the meat nice and juicy. Then slice the roast beef thinly and arrange on plates. Serve with a horseradish dip and a French stick with herb butter.

Roast Pork Bavarian Style

2 lbs (1 kg) pork from the shoulder with skin

salt

pepper

oil to grease the oven-proof dish

1 tsp caraway seeds

1 tsp dried marjoram,
1 tsp dried thyme and
1 tsp dried basil

1 pint (500 ml) real ale

2 lbs (1 kg) Spanish onions

herbs for decoration

Preparation time: approx. 30 minutes
(plus baking time)
Per serving: approx. 662 cals/2782 kj

1 Preheat the oven to gas mark 4 (350° F or 180° C). Wash and dry the shoulder of pork and score with criss-cross cuts using a sharp knife. Rub the skin with salt and pepper.

2 Grease an oven-proof dish with the oil. Place the meat with the skin upward onto the baking tray and sprinkle with the caraway seeds and herbs. Add the beer. Peel and chop the onions and add to the baking tray.

3 Place in the centre of the oven and for approximately 80 minutes. Braise every now and then with the beer. Brush the beer sauce onto the crust and switch on the oven grill 10 minutes before the end.

An alternative to our serving suggestion would be to accompany Bavarian roast pork with bretzels and sweet mustard. A tasty dark wheatbeer would round off the meal nicely.

4 At the end of the baking time switch off the oven, open the door and leave the meat to rest for approximately 10 minutes so it gets nice and juicy. After 10 minutes slice the meat, arrange on plates and garnish with the herbs. Serve with mashed potatoes and sauerkraut.

Oven Baked Salmon Trout

1 cleaned and gutted salmon
trout (approximately 3 lbs/
1 1/2 kg)

1 tbsp lemon juice

salt

pepper

6 stalks celery

8 tomatoes

5 oz (150 g) frozen herb mixture

3 oz (80 g) butter

1 fl oz (2 cl) whiskey

Preparation time: approx. 20 minutes
(plus baking time)
Per serving: approx. 485 cals/2037 kj

1 Preheat the oven to gas mark 4 (350° F
or 180° C). Wash and dry the fish and
sprinkle with lemon juice. Season with salt
and pepper. Wash the celery and cut
into smallish pieces.

2 Wash and halve the tomatoes. Remove
the green around the stalk and quarter
twice over. Defrost the herbs and mix
3 1/2 oz (100 g) together with the
tomatoes.

3 Stuff the trout with all the ingredients. Secure with wooden toothpicks. Grease aluminium foil with 1 oz (20 g) of the butter and place the trout on top. Sprinkle over the whiskey, flake the rest of the butter and place on the trout.

4 Sprinkle the rest of the herbs over the fish and wrap the trout in the foil. Place the fish in the centre of the oven and bake for approximately 20 minutes. Serve with wild and brown rice.

This is how you bone a whole fish: place it onto your working surface and make an incision from head to tail along the backbone using a sharp knife. Ease the fillet facing you off the rib bones with a knife. Then lift the backbone and loosen it from the flesh. Head and tail will be removed automatically and can be discarded together with the backbone.

Feel Free to Experiment

You have visitors coming – no problem. In this chapter you will find instructions and ideas that will leave you hardly able to wait for that relaxing evening with friends, turbulent parties or three-course meals that fill the whole evening for the demanding guests. But you need not fear even such baptism of fire!

Three-Course-Meal for Beginners

Wine and Herb Soup

3 onions

1 clove of garlic

7 oz (200 g) frozen herb mixture

4 tbsp butter

1 pint veal stock

1 pint (500 ml) white wine

salt, pepper

ground nutmeg

4 tbsp crème fraîche

2 eggs

4 tbsp croutons

Preparation time: approx. 15 minutes
Per serving: approx. 340 cals/1431 kj

1 Peel and dice the onions. Peel and crush the clove of garlic. Defrost the herbs.

2 Melt the butter in a pan and sauté the onions, garlic and herb mixture. After about 3 minutes add the veal stock and the white wine and season with salt, pepper and ground nutmeg. Leave to simmer on a low flame for approximately 5 minutes.

3 Preheat the oven to gas mark 4 (350° F or 180° C). Turn down the flame so the soup has stopped boiling before stirring in the crème fraîche. Separate the eggs and beat the egg whites until stiff.

4 Stir the egg yolks into the soup. Spread the stiff egg whites over the soup and bake in the oven for approximately 8 minutes. Decorate with croutons and serve.

Marinaded Fillets of Pork

1 red onion

2 green chilli peppers

2 cloves of garlic

3 tbsp herb mustard

salt, 3 tbsp basil

1 tbsp ground caraway

1 tbsp ground coriander

1 tsp paprika

3 tbsp raspberry vinegar

4 tbsp walnut oil

1 1/4 lbs (600 g) fillet of pork

pepper

1 1/2 lbs (750 g) green beans

2 tbsp herb butter

Preparation time: approx. 50 minutes
Per serving: approx. 380 cals/598 kj

1 Peel and dice the onions. Wash and halve the chilli peppers, deseed and cut into strips. Peel and crush the clove of garlic.

2 Transfer the onions, chillies, garlic, mustard, salt and chopped basil to a bowl and mix well. Season with the ground caraway, ground coriander and paprika. Stir in the oil and vinegar.

3 Wash and dry the meat. Rub in salt and pepper and cut into slices. Place in the marinade and leave to steep for 30 minutes.

4 In the meantime clean, wash and dry the beans and cook in slightly salted boiling water for approximately 4 minutes. Take the meat out of the marinade and fry in a non-stick pan for some 6 minutes.

5 Drain the beans using a sieve, transfer to a bowl and add the herb butter. Leave to melt on the hot beans. Arrange the meat on plates, add the vegetables and serve. Fried potatoes make for an ideal accompaniment to this dish.

Vanilla Ice Cream with Hot Cherries

1 1/4 lbs (600 g) preserved sour cherries

1 fl oz (2 cl) Kirsch

3 tbsp cherry jam

cornflour

8 small scoops vanilla ice cream

lemon balm for decoration

Preparation time: approx. 10 minutes
Per serving: approx. 243 cals/1023 kj

1 Place a sieve over a pot and drain the cherries. Add the Kirsch and cherry jam to the pot and heat on a very low flame.

2 Mix the cornflour with some water and add to the pot. Bring to the boil and take off the flame immediately. Stir in the cherries carefully. Transfer the sauce onto plates, add the vanilla ice cream scoops and cherries. Decorate with lemon balm and serve.

Fabulous Festive Menu

Avocado and Goat's Cheese Cocktail

8 small slices of goat's cheese

3 tbsp maple syrup

salt

pepper

4 tbsp raspberry vinegar

4 tbsp pumpkin seeds

4 avocado pears

3 tbsp lemon juice

Preparation time: approx. 15 minutes
Per serving: approx. 697 cals/2930 kj

1 Dice the goat's cheese and transfer into a bowl. Sprinkle with the maple syrup and season with salt and pepper. Mix together the oil and vinegar and pour over the mixture. Coarsely chop the pumpkin seeds and fry in a frying pan without any oil or butter. Add to the cheese mixture.

2 Halve the avocado pears, remove the stones and scoop out the flesh to within 1/2 inch of the peel. Sprinkle with the lemon juice. Dice the scooped out avocado flesh and add to the cheese mixture. Transfer the mixture into the avocado pears and serve.

Veal, Rolled and Stuffed with Savoy Cabbage

2 lbs shoulder of veal (have your butcher cut it into slices for roulades), salt, pepper

10 oz (300 g) veal sausage

3 1/2 oz (100 g) tomato purée

2 tbsp grain mustard

2 tbsp breadcrumbs

3 1/2 oz (100 g) fresh or frozen Italian herbs

4 tbsp clarified butter

1/4 pint (150 ml) veal stock

1/4 pint (150 ml) red wine

2 lbs (1 kg) savoy cabbage

2 Spanish onions

3 tbsp butter

1/4 pint (150 ml) vegetable stock

3 1/2 oz (100 g) sour cream ground caraway

Preparation time: approx. 80 minutes
Per serving: approx. 830 cals/3488 kj

1 Spread the meat out on a working surface and season. Take the meat from the veal sausage and mix with the tomato purée. Add the mustard, breadcrumbs and the chopped herbs and season. Cover the meat with the mixture, roll up and secure with yarn.

2 Melt the clarified butter in a pan and brown the roulades on all sides.

3 Add the veal stock and red wine after about 8 minutes and simmer for about 1 hour.

4 Wash, halve and remove the core from the savoy cabbage. Cut the rest into strips. Peel and dice the onions. Sauté the savoy cabbage and onions in a pan. Season with salt and pepper.

5 After about 3 minutes add the vegetable stock and simmer for another 7 minutes. Stir in the sour cream and season with salt, pepper and the ground caraway. Slice the meat, arrange on plates together with vegetables and serve with duchess potatoes.

Pineapple Fritters

12 slices tinned pineapple

3 1/2 oz (100 g) ground almonds

3 1/2 oz (100 g) breadcrumbs

1/2 tsp ground ginger, 1/2 tsp ground cardamom and 1/2 tsp ground cloves

2 eggs

3 tbsp butter

13 oz (400 g) natural yoghurt

Preparation time: approx. 10 minutes
Per serving: approx. 522 cals/2192 kj

1 Drain the pineapple slices saving the juice. Mix together the ground almonds, breadcrumbs and spices. Whisk the eggs. Dip the pineapple slices into the egg and then into the breadcrumb mixture.

2 Brown the pineapple slices in a pan. Mix together the juice and natural yoghurt. Arrange the pineapple slices and yoghurt mixture on plates and serve.

Spanish Menu

Sangria

2 apples

2 lemons

1 orange

1 grapefruit

3 1/2 oz (100 g) brown sugar

2 tbsp vanilla sugar

2 pints (1 l) Spanish red wine

1 fl oz (2 cl) cognac or brandy

1 pint (500 ml) mineral water

Preparation time: approx. 10 minutes (plus steeping time)
Per serving: approx. 167 cals/703 kj

1 Wash, peel, halve and core the apples. Cut into thin strips.

2 Peel the lemons, orange and grapefruit. Remove the white skin and divide into segments.

3 Transfer the fruit into a large jug and add the brown sugar and vanilla sugar. Pour the red wine and cognac or brandy into the jug, stir and leave to steep for approximately 2 hours in the refrigerator.

4 Just before serving, add the ice cold mineral water. Transfer into long drink glasses, decorate with fruit slices and serve.

Paella

7 oz (200 g) breast of chicken

7 oz (200 g) fillet of pork

3 onions

2 cloves of garlic

2 red peppers

7 oz (200 g) clams from a glass

4 tomatoes

3 1/2 oz (100 g) chorizo (Spanish sausage) or salami

6 tbsp peanut oil

10 oz (300 g) paella or risotto rice

2 tins saffron

1 tbsp curcuma

2 tbsp paprika

1 tbsp chilli powder

12 fl oz (350 ml) vegetable stock

1/4 pint (125 ml) dry white wine

7 oz (200 g) cooked shrimps

3 1/2 oz (100 g) frozen peas

salt, pepper

lemon slices for decoration

Preparation time: approx. 25 minutes (plus baking time)
Per serving: approx. 905 cals/3801 kj

1 Preheat the oven to gas mark 4 (350° F or 180° C). Wash, dry and dice the meat. Peel and dice the onions. Peel and crush the cloves of garlic.

2 Wash and dry the red peppers. Cut in half lengthwise, remove the stalk and deseed. Cut into strips. Drain the clams in a sieve.

3 Wash, dry and cut the tomatoes in half. Remove the green around the stem and quarter twice over. Cut the sausage into strips.

4 Heat the oil in a pan and brown the meat for approximately 6 minutes. Remove the meat and set aside.

5 Sauté the onions, garlic and pepper strips in the pan.

6 Add the uncooked risotto or paella rice and season with the seasonings. Add the stock and red wine. Transfer in the centre of the oven and bake for approximately 15 minutes.

7 When the liquid is evaporated add the sausage, clams, meat and the defrosted peas and cook for a further 8 minutes.

8 Season with salt and pepper prior to serving. Arrange on plates and decorate with the lemon slices.

There is no one recipe for the real Spanish paella. You can use whatever ingredients you happen to have at your disposal. The most important basis is the golden yellow saffron rice.

Prague Menu

Savoury Beetroot

1 1/4 lbs (600 g) cooked beetroot

3 tbsp raspberry vinegar

6 tbsp pumpkin seed oil

salt

pepper

1 tsp caraway seeds

8 oz (250 g) cream cheese

5 tbsp single cream

watercress for decoration

Preparation time: approx. 10 minutes (plus steeping time)
Per serving: approx. 331 cals/1391 kj

1 Wash, dry and dice the beetroot. Transfer into a bowl. Mix together the pumpkin seed oil, raspberry vinegar, salt, pepper and caraway seeds and pour over the beetroot. Leave to steep for approximately 20 minutes.

2 In a separate bowl mix together the cream cheese and single cream. Then stir the mousse into the beetroot. Arrange on glass plates and decorate with the watercress.

You do not normally store oil in the refrigerator as it tends to solidify. Perishable oils such as pumpkin seed oil, however, must be kept cold. The fact that it does tend to solidify does not have adverse effects on the taste. It just does not look quite so good. You should use up the oil as quickly as possible.

Gammon Prague Style

1 lb (500 g) farmhouse bread mix

1 tbsp caraway seeds

flour to spread on the working surface

1 1/4 lbs (600 g) smoked gammon (in one piece)

7 oz (200 g) ready made basil pesto

4 tbsp breadcrumbs

1/4 pint (125 g) lager beer

Preparation time: approx. 30 minutes (plus baking time)
Per serving: approx. 785 cals/3297 kj

1 Preheat the oven to gas mark 4 (350° F or 180° C). Prepare the bread mix following the instructions and kneed in the caraway seeds. Sprinkle the flour onto your working surface and roll out the dough until it is about 12 x 15 inches (30 x 40 cm) big.

2 Place the gammon in the middle of the dough. Mix together the basil pesto, breadcrumbs and beer. Spread the entire mixture over the gammon.

3 Fold up the dough. Make sure you whet and press together the edges. Put grease-proof paper in a baking tray and transfer the gammon onto the paper.

4 Bake in the oven for about 50 minutes. Braise the surface every now and then with beer to make it crispy.

5 After you have taken the meat out of the oven leave to rest for about 6 minutes. Then slice and arrange on plates. Boiled potatoes and a cold lager make for an ideal accompaniment.

Summit of Scrumptiousness

Desserts, biscuits, cakes: what would a festive dinner be without a proper dessert? Complete your first culinary steps with our summits of scrumptiousness. Sorbets or mousses, fruity desserts or simply "la dolce vita": vary how you see fit and how you want your guests to remember you. Or why not celebrate your successful entry into the culinary world by finishing it all off with a tasty delight?

Spicy Sorbet

2 pints (1 l) red wine

8 oz (250 g) pineapple slices

8 oz (250 g) tinned tangerines

1 untreated lemon

5 oz (150 g) brown cane sugar

2 bags mulled wine seasoning

lemon balm for decoration

Preparation time: approx. 25 minutes
(plus freezing time)
Per serving: approx. 481 cals/2021 kj

1 Transfer the wine into a pot and add the diced pineapple slices and tangerines including the liquid. Wash and dry the lemon. Slice thinly and add together with the brown cane sugar to the wine.

2 Bring to the boil and leave to simmer on a low heat for approximately 6 minutes. Add the mulled wine seasoning and leave to simmer for a further 5 minutes.

3 Now strain the liquid into a bowl using a sieve. Wait for it to cool and place in the freezer for approximately 6 hours. Give it a whisk with a fork every now and then.

4 Transfer the sorbet into dessert bowls and garnish with fruit and lemon balm.

You can prepare sorbet with almost any fruit and liquid. However, you can also buy ice cream sorbet such as lemon ice cream, mix it with sparkling wine or vodka and freeze it for a short while.

Pear Compote

4 pears

1/2 pint (250 g) rosé

1 fl oz (2 cl) raspberry brandy

4 tbsp brown cane sugar

3 tbsp butter

4 tbsp breadcrumbs

4 tbsp sour cream

lemon balm for decoration

Preparation time: approx. 30 minutes
Per serving: approx. 328 cals/1380 kj

1 Wash and peel the pears. Cut in half lengthwise. Core and dice. Transfer the wine and raspberry brandy to a pot and add the pears. Leave to steep on a low flame for approximately 8 minutes.

2 Preheat the oven to gas mark 4 (350° F or 180° C). Squash the pears with a fork and transfer to four small oven-proof soufflé dishes. Mix the cane sugar with the breadcrumbs and sprinkle over the dishes.

3 Sprinkle with flakes of butter and place in the centre of the oven. Bake for approximately 15 minutes. Decorate with 1 tablespoon of sour cream and a few leaves of the lemon balm and serve.

Rice Pudding with Blueberries

**1 lb (500 g)
blueberries**

2 pints (1 l) milk

2 tbsp butter

**2 tbsp can
sugar**

1 tsp vanilla powder

1 tsp ground cinnamon

8 oz (250 g) pudding rice

lemon balm for decoration

Preparation time: approx. 30 minutes
Per serving: approx. 587 cals/2465 kj

1 Wash and dry the blueberries. Transfer the milk and butter into a pan. Add the sugar, vanilla powder and ground cinnamon and bring to the boil.

2 Add the pudding rice and leave to simmer on a low flame for approximately 20 minutes. The rice is ready when all the milk has been absorbed. Arrange on plates and place the blueberries on top.

3 Decorate the rice pudding with a sprinkle of the cane sugar, cinnamon and lemon balm. You can serve this dish both warm and cold.

White Mousse with Chocolate

4 eggs

3 1/2 oz (100 g) brown
cane sugar

1 tbsp vanilla sugar

3 1/2 fl oz (100 ml) orange
juice

2 tbsp orange liqueur

1 pint (500 ml) instant
chocolate sauce

7 tbsp whipped cream

whipped cream
for decoration

lemon balm for decoration

Preparation time: approx. 20 minutes
Per serving: approx. 735 cals/ 3087 kJ

1 Separate the eggs. Transfer the egg yolks, half the sugar and vanilla powder into a bowl and mix well. Slowly pour in the orange juice while stirring continuously.

2 Fill a large pot half with water and put on the heat. Place the bowl with the egg mixture in the pot and stir until the mixture is warm and creamy. Whisk the egg whites with the remaining sugar until stiff.

3 Add the orange liqueur and carefully fold the whisked egg whites in the egg yolk mixture. Prepare the chocolate sauce following the instructions on the packet and add the whipped cream.

4 Transfer the cream into dessert bowls and pour over the chocolate sauce. Decorate with a little whipped cream and lemon balm.

When leafing through recipes, you will probably come across the terms vanilla sugar or vanilla powder. These are two different substances, the former being the "real thing" and as such very aromatic. It is also somewhat more expensive than its artificial cousin.

"Dolce Vita" Choux Buns

2 mangos

1 fl oz (2 cl) almond liqueur

13 oz (400 g) cream cheese

2 sachets vanilla sugar

7 oz (200 g) yoghurt

3 tbsp single cream

3 tbsp flaked almonds

16 little frozen Italian choux buns

3 tbsp apricot jam

1/2 bunch lemon balm for decoration

Preparation time: approx. 25 minutes
Per serving: approx. 407 cals/1712 kj

1 Peel and half the mangos lengthwise. Remove the stone and dice the mango flesh. Sprinkle with the almond liqueur and leave to steep for approximately 10 minutes.

2 In the meantime transfer the cream cheese with the vanilla sugar, yoghurt and single cream into a bowl and mix well. Roast the flaked almonds in a frying pan without any oil or butter. Fold the mangos in the cream cheese mixture.

3 Take the choux buns and remove the upper half. Place the cream cheese mixture on the lower halves and replace the tops.

4 Cover the tops with the apricot jam and sprinkle with the flaked almonds. Arrange on a platter and serve.

The crispy small choux buns from Italy are called "bignè".
You will find them in well-stocked supermarkets.
These handy little sweets can quickly and very easily be filled with fruit, pudding or other treats.
Once you have acquired the taste, you will find it hard to let go...

Creamy Peach Slices

flour to sprinkle on the working surface

12 oz (350 g) frozen puff pastry

1 lb (500 g) tinned peaches

10 oz (300 g) creamy curd cheese

3 tbsp rum

1 tbsp lemon juice

3 1/2 oz (100 g) chocolate flake

Preparation time: approx. 25 minutes
Per serving: approx. 692 cals/2909 kj

1 Sprinkle the flour over your working surface. Place the defrosted slices of dough on top of one another and cut into 12 rectangles. Place a sieve over a bowl and drain the peaches in the sieve, catching the juice in the bowl.

2 Place grease-proof paper on a baking tray and preheat the oven to gas mark 7 (425° F or 220° C). Transfer the puff pastry rectangles onto the baking tray, leaving small spaces in between.

3 Now pierce the rectangles all over with a fork and put in the centre of the oven. Bake for approximately 15 minutes. In the meantime cut the peaches into small pieces and mix together with the curd cheese.

4 Add the rum and the lemon juice. Should the curd cheese mixture not be smooth enough simply add some liquid from the tinned peaches. Leave the puff pastry to cool and spread the curd cheese mixture onto half the rectangles. Crumble up the chocolate flake and sprinkle over the curd cheese mixture. Cover with the other rectangles and serve.

You can also use a variety of other fruits for the filling such as tangerines, strawberries or lychees. A nice final touch is to serve the slices with whipped cream.

Grape and Sour Cream Pie

5 tbsp grape juice,
13 oz (400 g) black grapes

1 fl oz (2 oz) brandy

4 eggs, 3 1/2 oz (100 g) cornflour

1 lb (500 g) sour cream, 2 tbsp
single cream

1/2 tsp ground aniseed, 1/2 tsp
ground ginger, 1/2 tsp ground
cloves

butter to grease the
oven-proof dish

2 oz (50 g) sunflower seeds

*Preparation time: approx. 15 minutes
(plus baking time)
Per serving: approx. 629 cals/2644 kj*

1 Wash, halve and deseed the grapes. Transfer to a bowl. Sprinkle the juice and brandy over the grapes and leave to steep for approximately 10 minutes. Preheat the oven to gas mark 4 (350° F or 180° C).

2 In the meantime break the eggs into a bowl and add the cornflour. Mix together the sour cream and single cream, season with the spices and add everything to the eggs.

3 Grease a pie dish with the butter and pour in the mixture. Smoothen and sprinkle with the grapes and sunflower seeds. Place in the centre of the oven and bake for approximately 50 minutes. Leave to cool and serve warm.

Crunchy Oat Macaroons

5 oz (150 g) wholemeal oats

5 oz (150 g) butter

1 tbsp orange peel aroma

3 eggs, 5 oz (150 g) cane sugar

1 1/2 oz (40 g) vanilla sugar,
5 tbsp maple syrup, 1 tsp baking
powder, 7 oz (200 g) flour

1/2 tsp ground cinnamon, 1/2 tsp
ground cardamom, 1/2 tsp
ground aniseed, 7 oz
(200 g) chopped walnuts

icing sugar

Preparation time: approx. 25 minutes
Per serving: approx. 1133 cals/4758 kj

1 Fry the wholemeal oats together with the butter and the orange peel aroma for approximately 3 minutes, stirring continuously. Crack the eggs into a bowl and add the sugar, vanilla sugar and maple syrup. Whisk well.

2 Add the wholemeal oats to the egg mixture and then add the baking powder, flour and spices. Stir in the chopped walnuts. Cover a baking tray with grease-proof paper. Transfer the mixture onto the paper with a spoon, making small heaps.

3 Leave at room temperature for approximately 30 minutes. Preheat the oven to gas mark 4 (350° F or 180° C) and place the baking tray in the centre of the oven. Bake for approximately 15 minutes. Sprinkle with icing sugar and serve.